WHAT'S A GERM, JOSEPH LISTER?

WHAT'S A

GERM,

JOSEPH LISTER?

**The Medical Mystery
That Forever Changed
the Way We Heal**

LORI ALEXANDER

ILLUSTRATIONS BY
DANIEL DUNCAN

Clarion Books
An Imprint of HarperCollins*Publishers*

Clarion Books is an imprint of HarperCollins Publishers.

What's a Germ, Joseph Lister?
Text copyright © 2023 by Lori Alexander
Art copyright © 2023 by Daniel Duncan

Library of Congress Control Number: 2023933838
ISBN 978-0-35-853817-2

Typography by Torborg Davern
23 24 25 26 27   GPS   10 9 8 7 6 5 4 3 2 1

First Edition

To pioneering scientists and doctors,

who move the world forward with careful research

and dogged determination

—L. A.

For the little one

—D. D.

Contents

- Hippocrates -

The physician must . . . have two special
objects in view with regard to disease,
namely, to do good or to do no harm.

—HIPPOCRATES, GREEK PHYSICIAN
(460–375 BCE)

- Joseph Lister -

I am fitted to be a surgeon: for thou canst
hardly conceive what a high degree of
enjoyment I am from day to day experiencing
in this bloody and butchering department of
the healing art.

—DR. JOSEPH LISTER
(1827–1912)

Introduction

When eleven-year-old James Greenlees stepped into traffic on August 12, 1865, he had no idea he would make medical history.

As it did most days, the growing city of Glasgow, Scotland, bustled with activity. Workers rushed to jobs at the shipyard, the textile factory, the coal mine. Pedestrians made their way to the market. Horses pulled carriages packed with people or goods.

Clomping hooves and rattling wheels were nothing new for James. So maybe he wasn't paying enough attention when he tried to cross the busy road. A horse lugging an empty wooden cart knocked James off his feet. One of the metal-rimmed wheels rolled over his left leg, leaving a bloody gash below his knee.

James screamed. The driver stopped. Passersby gathered and gasped. Was the leg broken? Definitely. The splintered bone poked through the open wound on his shin. James needed treatment from the local hospital.

This was the worst news of all.

CHAPTER 1

A Painful History

In the early 1800s, hospitals were not the clean, quiet life-saving places we know today. Rats scurried across filthy floors. Lice lived in unwashed bedsheets. Screams echoed down dimly lit halls. The smells of blood, vomit, and rotting flesh lingered in the stuffy air. Back then, the idea of a hospital visit caused fear and dread.

Why were hospitals so dirty, loud, and foul-smelling?

In Glasgow and many other rapidly growing cities in Europe and the United States, basic cleanliness was a struggle. Large families lived in tiny, crowded homes. Water for cooking and cleaning had to be carried inside from a public well. Most people bathed only a few times a year. Toilets were nothing more than a wooden seat above a backyard drain. Waste flowed into a cesspool, an underground brick-lined pit. Often, this waste would seep into the soil and pollute the well water, which was also used for drinking.

Outside, garbage piled high along sidewalks. Roads grew slick with muck from the urine and manure left by thousands of working horses. Skies grayed with smog from factory smokestacks. Manufacturing and mining jobs were plentiful, but they were also dangerous. Workers breathed toxic air day after day. Fingers, hands, arms, and legs were easily mangled in machinery accidents.

With so many ways for people to become ill or injured, hospitals were overloaded. Doctors had hundreds of patients to see each day. Men, women, and children—their grimy boots and long dresses dragging in the dirt off the streets—waited for hours before they received any attention.

Hazardous Hospitals

In the 1600s and 1700s, hospitals were built mainly to treat the poor. When great outbreaks of disease occurred, hospitals filled up quickly. Many patients had to share beds. Those who could afford it would pay a doctor to come to their home instead. In the early 1800s, mortality rates for operations were up to five times lower when treatment took place at home. You were much more likely to survive a surgery on your dining room table than at your local hospital.

To make matters worse, doctors didn't yet understand how diseases spread from one person to the next. They knew very little about the way the human body worked. No treatment existed for contagious infections such as smallpox, cholera, and pneumonia. Most treatments were a mixture of herbs and superstition. These potions and pills did little to cure people of their symptoms. In fact, many treatments did more harm than good.

Start the Bleeding

Until the mid-1800s, it didn't matter if you had a fever, sore throat, cough, allergies, headache, stomachache, pneumonia, seizures, or smallpox. Most doctors would try one treatment before any other: bloodletting. Doctors believed that illnesses were caused by bad blood or too much blood in the body. The most popular remedy was to cut a patient's vein and allow the blood to fill a bowl. This bleeding did little to heal the patient and could be deadly if too much blood was taken or if the incision became infected. Without a solid understanding of disease, this harsh treatment was in place for more than two thousand years.

A doctor would schedule a surgery only for the most urgent cases. With no drugs to block pain, operations took place while patients were wide awake! Screams of terror filled hospital halls. Dirty bandages covered oozing incisions. Doctors washed their hands *after* a procedure, not before. If a person was lucky enough to survive surgery, she'd likely die from an infection in the recovery ward. For these reasons, hospitals were commonly referred to as "houses of death."

Who could rid hospitals of this filth and fear?

CHAPTER 2

The Boy and the Bones

Joseph Lister slipped out the back door. He ran until he reached the wooded area behind his country home. Birds chirped. Insects hummed. And Joseph searched for treasures.

Born into a large Quaker family in a village about ten miles east of London, Joseph was one of seven children. Being Quaker meant his family lived a simple and peaceful life. They did not play sports or go hunting. They did not listen to music or take trips to the theater. Joseph enjoyed drawing and painting. His home was filled with books, and there was plenty of time for reading. His house even had a mini museum—a small room of shelves and cabinets that

WHAT'S A GERM, JOSEPH LISTER?

displayed fossils, leaves, rocks, and insects. Would Joseph find something today to add to his family's collection?

Joseph's father was also curious about nature and science. He had left school at age fourteen to learn the trade of wine merchant but had developed a keen interest in microscopes.

In the 1820s, people were frustrated with microscopes. The tool had been invented more than two hundred years earlier. In the late 1600s, Antony van Leeuwenhoek used microscopes to discover red blood cells, muscle fibers, even tiny living organisms that would later be known as bacteria. But currently, microscopes were little more than gadgets to entertain the wealthy. Few people used them for scientific purposes. Part of the problem was that the glass lenses inside the device made samples look blurry and purple around the edges (an issue called *chromatic distortion*). Still working at his wine business, Joseph's father had learned to grind his own lenses and solved this problem. He taught other scientists how to make the improved lenses. And he used the newly perfected microscope to make some discoveries of his own.

Joseph stood on his tiptoes and peeked into his father's microscope. An oak leaf. A pinch of soil. The eye of a fly. Each item had secrets to reveal, a world of tiny details hidden to the naked eye. Little did Joseph know, the microscope would become an important tool in his own future.

At age eleven Joseph moved to a Quaker boarding school about fifty miles from home, just as his older brothers had done before him. The thought of leaving his family made Joseph's stomach ache. Worse still, whenever he felt nervous or anxious, he spoke with a stutter that caused him much embarrassment.

Once settled, Joseph wrote to his mother and father about his new schedule:

> We get up at six, and have two hours [of class] before breakfast and another quarter of an hour at half past eleven; we go down from school to dinner, have half an hour after dinner, and an hour and a half of school in the afternoon; we

have supper at half past six, bread and cheese
and beer on fourth and seventh days, and bread
and butter and milk and water on the other days.

Joseph excelled at math and science. He was slower when it came to writing essays. And he complained about too much spelling and grammar practice. But Joseph received good reports from his teacher: "He finds no difficulty in his learning and I hope is making good progress." After three years Joseph moved to a different Quaker school for more advanced studies. Always on the quiet side, Joseph tried his best to hide his stutter, noting "the boys do not even know . . . as the Master did not tell anyone."

In 1841, fourteen-year-old Joseph was home for summer break. Sitting in his bedroom without much to do, he reached for a pencil and paper. Slowly he sketched a human hand. Then he added all of the bones. Later he drew a human skeleton and painted on red muscles.

Growing more curious about the way bodies work, Joseph sliced open a fish's belly to study its insides. Next

he dissected the head of a sheep. "I got almost all the meat off," Joseph told his father, after removing the sheep's

brain and cleaning off the skull. Joseph also dissected a frog. He peeled away the skin and carefully removed the muscles and organs. Then he snuck a piece of wood out of the family museum, a treasure his sister Mary had found. On it, Joseph mounted the skeleton. "It looks just as if it was going to take a leap." He proudly displayed the frog on the top shelf. Joseph couldn't wait to show his father but pleaded, "Do not tell Mary about the piece of wood."

Summer vacation was now over. Joseph knew what he wanted to do next. He wanted to become a surgeon.

CHAPTER 3

The Quick or the Dead

Joseph's father wasn't pleased with this decision. Most Quakers believed that under God's protective care the body would heal itself without hospitals or human meddling. Joseph's father preferred "to let Nature do her own work." Besides that, surgery was not the highly skilled and respected career we know today. A surgeon's job was dirty and dangerous, and they made very little money.

Before the 1800s there was a big difference between a doctor and a surgeon.

Doctors required medical training at a university. They were admired for their wisdom. But surgeons needed no degree or special schooling. They typically learned by watching other surgeons, much like an apprentice learning a new trade. The job of surgeon was grouped into the same category as any other job that involved working with one's hands, not much different from a barber or a butcher.

The Barber-Surgeon

 While doctors were quick to prescribe bloodletting for most conditions, they believed they were too educated to cut into flesh. That was the messy job of a surgeon. Early surgeons, dating back to 1000 CE, began as barbers. Trimming hair and shaving beards made them experts with sharp blades. Barbers soon took on the tasks of opening veins for bleeding, removing warts, and pulling teeth. The striped barber pole is thought to represent white cloth bandages stained red from

bloodletting. Beginning in 1745, British laws sepa-rated the roles of surgeons and barbers. Surgeons began to receive more and better training.

Most early surgeons knew surprisingly little about the insides of the human body. And before 1846 there were no effective medicines to help patients with pain during an operation. With patients wide awake, surgery on the brain, spine, heart, or any other organ was impossible. For these reasons, most surgeries were fairly minor: stitching up a cut or removing a cyst or wart.

But in a time when cleanliness was diffi-cult, even small injuries such as scratch-es, burns, or cuts could lead to death. Bacteria entered the wound and caused infection to spread. Unfortunately, doctors didn't know about bac-teria yet. They didn't use the

word *infection* either. They called it **sepsis**, from the Greek word meaning "decay" or "rot." Doctors **did** know a red, swollen wound could quickly turn "septic," leaving a patient with pain and a high fever. Their wound would likely fill with pus or even turn black, a sign of a dangerous disease called gangrene. If left unchecked, gangrene spread into the blood and vital organs. A simple scratch could become a matter of life or death.

To stop sepsis, there was only one thing a surgeon could do—cut off the entire body part. In the early 1800s, amputation was a common surgical procedure. To remove a hand, foot, or even an entire arm or leg, a surgeon needed two basic skills: speed and strength.

Setting the Stage

In the early 1800s, operations were often performed in front of an audience. Doctors, assistants, and medical students packed into the first rows of the operating theater. Curious townspeople could watch as well. They were there not to learn surgical skills but to be entertained by the drama and horror. The theater was located on the top floor of the hospital. Before electric lights, invented in 1879, most procedures were scheduled for midday, when the sun filtered through the skylights high above. A row of sharp knives and saws, quickly wiped down after previous surgeries, lay

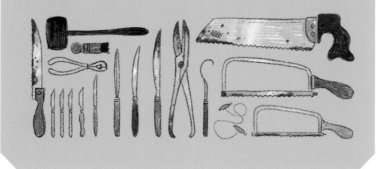

on a small stand near a stained wooden operating table. Sawdust covered the floor, ready to soak up puddles of blood, much as it was done at the town butcher shop.

Being cut into is scary. Without pain medicine, patients facing surgery were terrified. Most had to be strapped to the table or held down by strong assistants. The surgeon had to work quickly as patients started to thrash and wail before long. Many passed out from the pain, which was probably for the best.

Your Watches

In the 1840s, London surgeon Robert Liston was known as "the fastest knife in the West End." At the beginning of an amputation he shouted into the audience, "Time me, gentlemen!" In one swift move, he sliced through skin and muscle. Then he placed the bloody knife between his teeth and grabbed his saw. With a few quick stokes, the infected limb fell away. Liston tied off blood vessels with a length of thread he had waiting in the buttonhole of his coat. From first cut to final stitch, it took Liston thirty seconds.

Surgery's dirty and dangerous history did not sway Joseph away from his goal. He made a deal with his father. Joseph would earn a college degree before training to be a surgeon. In 1844, at the age of seventeen, he moved to the city and began taking classes at University College London.

CHAPTER 4

Easing the Pain

Compared with the bright open spaces of his country home, the busy city felt cramped and gloomy to Joseph. He spent most of his time indoors, studying for classes in mathematics, chemistry, history, and languages such as French, German, and Latin. He made few friends. His roommate noted that Joseph "lived in the world of his thoughts." Was Joseph growing uncertain about his decision to become a surgeon?

On December 21, 1846, Joseph tagged along with one of his roommates, who promised they were about to see something special. At the nearby university hospital, Joseph jostled his way into the crowded operating theater.

Dr. Liston took the stage. Today he would perform a mid-thigh amputation. But instead of asking the audience to time his speedy work, he yelled to the crowd, "We are going to try a Yankee dodge today, gentlemen, for making men insensible!"

The patient twisted on the table. He took a breath from a special tube while an ether-soaked cloth was draped across his face. Before long, the patient went still. No struggling or screaming, like usual. Joseph and the rest of the crowd fell silent. The amputation took only twenty-five seconds. A few minutes later the patient woke and asked nervously, "When are you going to begin?" The crowd burst into laughter and applause.

Killing Pain

The "Yankee dodge" referred to a discovery made by William Morton, an American dentist, when he experimented with a compound called ether. When his patients inhaled the liquid's fumes, they could no longer feel the pain of having a tooth removed. The news of pain-free surgery quickly spread throughout America and Europe, where soon more surgeons were eager to give ether a try. Another liquid, called chloroform, was experimented with as well. It produced a similar effect but could put patients to sleep faster than ether did. With a relaxed patient, surgeons could now take more time operating.

Joseph became more interested in surgery than ever. In December 1847 he finished his classwork and passed his final tests. As the first person in his family to graduate from college, he received a special gift from his father—a microscope of his very own.

CHAPTER 5

Hospital Disease

In 1848 Joseph began medical school at University College London. He attended advanced classes in chemistry, physics, and botany. He also followed surgeons in the university's hospital, carrying supplies, taking notes and learning what he could from the operating theater to the recovery wards.

To better understand the human body and how all of its parts work together, Joseph took anatomy classes. Since only so much could be learned from his textbooks, his classes also included lessons in dissection, the act of cutting apart a dead body, or cadaver, to study its structure. Joseph already knew that a human body was much more complex than that of the fish and sheep and frog he had dissected as a boy.

Public Dissections

Medical students weren't the only ones interested in cadaver dissections. Beginning in the 1500s, ordinary citizens could be found watching these events. They were especially popular in Italy, where fewer laws prevented public dissection. Scented candles flickered and soft music played while a barber-surgeon sliced into a body, typically of an executed criminal or a poor citizen with no family. Artists sketched details of the scene. Some people fainted or swore they'd never return, though many dissections drew hundreds of viewers. They became such popular entertainment that some cities ran out of bodies. Gangs of "body snatchers" formed to steal freshly buried corpses from graveyards. While their actions were illegal, the robbers made a nice profit by selling the bodies to universities for public dissections or to medical schools *for anatomy classes. Today, strict laws are in place requiring that bodies dissected for medical science be donated by the owners themselves.*

Joseph became accustomed to the sights and strong smells in the school's dissecting room. He carefully cut through skin, fat, blood vessels, and muscles. With each new layer peeled back, the body shared its secrets. He studied slippery intestines and spongy lungs. Bits of brains and eyeballs. Medical students owed much of their learning to

these cadaver bodies. Indeed, it was thought that a young surgeon would "mangle the living if he has not operated on the dead."

In 1851 Joseph became an assistant to a more senior surgeon. He tended to patients, asked questions about their ailments, and took precise notes. For months he observed other surgeons as they worked on the sick and injured. Eventually, he was able to perform small surgeries under their supervision. What a thrill to help a suffering patient!

But this feeling didn't last long. While patients rested comfortably for a day or two after their surgery, soon many burned with fever. Their muscles ached. They stopped eating. When Joseph lifted a patient's soggy bandages, too often he found a stinking, pus-filled wound underneath. These rotting sores grew larger each day. The skin around the wound turned grayish black. Nearly half of the surgery patients were dying from gangrene or other septic diseases.

Why was this happening?

The senior surgeons had no good explanation. Some blamed *miasma* (from the Greek word meaning "pollution"), the theory that rotting sores created "bad air." It was thought that the odor spread throughout the hospital, making more patients sick. Joseph opened window after window to let in the fresh air. But this did little good. Some of the doctors joked that the foul-smelling air was part of the job, calling it "good old hospital stink."

Doctors grouped gangrene and the other septic illnesses that were killing patients into a single term: "hospital disease." Sadly, many doctors believed hospital disease
was an unavoidable part of surgery.

Joseph wasn't so sure. He scraped off a bit of a patient's
slimy sore and looked at it under his microscope. He saw
tiny rod-shaped particles. What were these? Could they

have something to do with his patients' deaths? Quickly, Joseph made a sketch. But when he showed the other surgeons his discovery, they were not impressed. They believed that the hospital existed for patient care only—it was not a place for research or microscopes.

By the end of 1852, Joseph had passed his final examinations with honors. He was fully qualified to practice surgery. But Joseph was still troubled by the death of so many patients. He wondered if doctors and surgeons were doing something wrong. To Joseph, "it seemed to be a lottery whether patients recovered or died."

What were they all missing? What more could Joseph do?

CHAPTER 6

Agnes and the Frogs

Months passed. Joseph made no plans for his future. Finally, one of his professors suggested that Joseph spend a month in Scotland working under James Syme, a well-known and highly skilled surgeon. After that Joseph could travel to other hospitals in Europe to gain more experience and learn about the latest medical practices. Joseph agreed to the plan. In September 1853 he settled in the city of Edinburgh and paid a visit to the famous surgeon Syme.

Joseph was quickly put to work. While Edinburgh was a smaller city than London, the hospital there was much larger. It held two hundred surgical beds, compared with the sixty at his old hospital. With more patients, there was more for Joseph to see and learn. Syme was an excellent teacher. He even allowed Joseph to choose which patients he wanted to treat: A dislocated ankle? A crushed hand? A knife wound to the neck?

In a letter to his father, Joseph wrote, "My present opportunities are teaching me what I could not learn from any books, nor indeed from anybody else."

But while the hospital in Edinburgh was bigger and better in many ways, it had the same problems as Joseph's old hospital. It was crowded and dirty. After surgery, nearly half of the patients died from hospital disease, just as they had in London.

Once again, Joseph took sore scrapings to view under his microscope. But what he really wanted to study was healthy tissue *before* hospital disease set in. Joseph knew the first sign of a worsening wound was often inflammation, redness and swelling of the skin. Was inflammation a normal part of healing? Or was it something that should be stopped?

Joseph decided to do an experiment on healthy skin to

see exactly how it went from normal to red and swollen. But he couldn't experiment on the patients. Outside his house, he found the perfect test subject.

Joseph carefully placed the frog under his microscope, focusing his lens on the frog's foot. The delicate webbing between the toes was so thin, Joseph could see blood moving through tiny blood vessels. He noted that the frog was "perfectly healthy" and "exceedingly quiet."

Next he placed a drop of warm water on the frog's foot. The blood vessels tightened, which stopped the blood from flowing. After a few seconds, the vessels opened and the blood began to flow even heavier than normal. Within a few more seconds, the frog's foot returned to normal. Joseph tried hotter and hotter water. He saw similar patterns. The hotter the water, the more the blood flowed in that area. All that extra blood explained why inflammation made skin looked red and swollen.

Now, instead of hot water, Joseph tried other irritants: small drops of various oils, acids, even mustard powder. He tried the mustard on his own arm as well. Each time, he watched the skin grow red and puffy and then return to normal. Joseph concluded that inflammation was a normal and important part of the healing process. But if the water was too hot or the chemicals were too strong, the healthy skin was destroyed. The blood could not flow into these tissues to fix the damage.

Joseph wondered if there was a connection between inflammation and hospital disease. His mind filled with ideas for more experiments. But he still had patients to see at the hospital. And now Joseph was asked to teach a surgery class to new medical students, giving weekly lectures and demonstrations. Joseph wished for more time. "If the day were twice as long, I should have abundant occupation

for it." In any free moments he continued his research with the frogs, hoping it would lead to answers for his patients.

Some evenings Joseph was invited to dine at Syme's home, located just outside the city. Set among grassy hills and flower gardens, the family dinners were a relaxing break from the bustle of the hospital. Joseph quickly took a liking to Syme's eldest daughter, Agnes. Agnes was fascinated by nature, science, and medicine. And maybe by Joseph as well.

On April 23, 1856, Joseph and Agnes were married. Using money they received as a wedding gift, they spent the following three months on a journey across Europe, visiting museums and scenic landmarks. But mostly they toured medical schools and hospitals, meeting the best surgeons in Belgium, Switzerland, Italy, Austria, Germany, and France. When they returned, Agnes became Joseph's lab partner. She took notes. She helped Joseph find the right words for his lectures and papers. And occasionally she chased down a runaway frog.

Women in Science in the 1800s

While Agnes Lister was not the only woman with an interest in science and medicine, very few women worked in these fields. At the time, most universities did not accept women. Many people believed that an education would interfere with a woman's role as wife and mother. Even after a few colleges began accepting female students in the late 1800s, it was difficult for women to

advance in scientific careers. Many could only find jobs assisting men. Some received no credit for their work or had to publish their research under their husbands' names. After Marie Curie won a second Nobel Prize in 1911, making her the first person to win twice, she was still not admitted into France's prestigious Academy of Sciences (the honor would not be bestowed on a woman until 1979). In the United States women make up about 43 percent of today's scientists and engineers. While this number is slowly rising, women currently face many of the same challenges as in the past, such as childcare needs, unequal pay, and lack of advancement to the highest ranks within universities and research labs.

Over the next three years Joseph published fifteen papers in scientific journals, many about the inflammation process he observed in the frogs' feet. In 1860 he accepted a position at the University of Glasgow, about forty miles from Edinburgh. There, Joseph would serve as professor of clinical surgery. In addition to teaching, he would apply for a surgery position at the nearby hospital. The surgery center was large, with more than five hundred beds. And better yet, it was brand new. Joseph hoped the building would be free of the dreaded hospital disease.

CHAPTER 7

A Medical Mystery

Joseph's footsteps clicked along the wooden floors of the new Glasgow Royal Infirmary. A cool breeze blew in from the large windows. Bed by bed, Joseph chatted with his patients. He fluffed pillows. He offered meals. He did his best to comfort those recovering from surgery. But something grim lurked beneath the sheets. Joseph unwrapped a bandage. The powerful reek of rotting flesh forced him to step back. Hospital disease had struck again!

Even more shocking, the other doctors believed these stinking, pus-filled wounds were a sign of normal healing. Joseph disagreed. Rotting wounds usually meant death wasn't far behind. He noted, "Whenever all, or nearly all, the beds contained cases with open sores, these grievous complications were sure to show themselves." The uncontrollable deaths weighed heavily on Joseph. "I have often felt ashamed, when recording results of my practice, to have so often to allude to hospital gangrene."

Joseph had noticed that most broken bones healed nicely. But if a broken bone tore through the skin, the wound rarely healed without pus and the spread of hospital disease. These "open fractures" almost always required an amputation. Even when this surgery was a success,

47

hospital disease could still attack during recovery. In the end, one out of every two surgery patients died.

Why did some injuries heal while others would not? Joseph vowed to solve this medical mystery.

Some doctors blamed the high death rate on miasma from the nearby graveyard. They thought the decomposing bodies were sending poisonous vapors into the hospital. Other doctors believed in **spontaneous generation**, the theory that living organisms can be made from nonliving things. They thought that deadly particles just appeared in the patients' wounds out of nowhere. Again, Joseph wasn't convinced.

Could cleanliness be the key? Joseph swept the hospital floors. He placed a few water basins in the operating theater and around his wards. But with many rotting wounds, most doctors still washed their hands *after* examining a patient, not before.

A Simple Solution

In 1847, a year before Joseph began medical school, Dr. Ignaz Semmelweis had a mystery on his hands. Young mothers were dying at Vienna General Hospital's maternity ward. Shortly after giving birth, they developed fever, pain, and swelling in their bellies. Sores spread across their bodies. Infection destroyed their internal organs. Few women recovered from the disease, called childbed *fever. Why was this happening? There were two maternity wards in the hospital. The first was run by male doctors and students and had a 20 percent death rate. The second was staffed by female midwives (assistants with no medical degree) and had only a 2 percent death rate. Were the new mothers afraid of the male doctors? Was it the bed linens? The air? Finally, Semmelweis made the connection. The doctors in the first ward had all spent time examining dead bodies before they delivered babies. The midwives never did. Semmelweis offered a simple solution: hand washing with a bleach-like solution. Unfortunately, many of his coworkers didn't think something as simple as hand washing could make a difference. They believed doctors were gentlemen and "a gentleman's hands are clean." With his research ignored, Semmelweis went mad and eventually died in a mental institution. It wasn't until decades later that his advice was recognized as correct.*

When it came to cleaning, Joseph never considered his attire. He operated in an old blue coat, the same one he wore while dissecting corpses. Like those of most doctors, Joseph's coat was crusted with blood and pus from previous surgeries. In fact, a well-stained coat was a sign of experience: "The stiffer the coat, the prouder the busy surgeon." Bare, unwashed fingers probed wounds. It was normal for doctors to use the same sponges and medical instruments from one patient to the next. Instruments were returned to their cases, typically without washing, even if they'd been dropped on the floor or used to amputate a limb.

After ten years of searching, Joseph was no closer to solving the mystery of hospital disease. The problem was as old as hospitals themselves. For hundreds of years people who entered with a mild condition or a simple wound left with a serious infection, if they left at all. An American military hospital reported that thousands of men admitted with slight injuries died from infections acquired during their hospital stay. "A soldier entering a great battle was in less danger than one entering the hospital."

The Lady with the Lamp

Florence Nightingale served as a British nurse in the Crimean War, a battle fought in the 1850s between Russia and an alliance of Britain, France, and Turkey. When she arrived at the military hospital, she found terrible conditions: overcrowding, low supplies, filthy bedsheets, rats, and fleas. She tended to wounded soldiers with kindness, throughout the day and by lamplight at night. She kept statistics on her patients and published her findings. Her graphs showed that more men died from disease than from battle. Nightingale implemented simple hygiene changes, such as hand washing. She also demanded supplies and cleaner facilities from the British government. After the war, in 1860, she formed the Nightingale School for Nurses. The blood, dirt, stench, and male body parts seen during nursing had once been considered inappropriate for women. But Nightingale gave the job a favorable reputation, teaching modern techniques and taking the role from lowly servant to medical professional. Joseph's wards were staffed with nurses trained by Nightingale beginning in 1873.

One afternoon near the end of 1864 a chemistry professor and friend of Joseph's mentioned some new research
happening in France. A scientist there had discovered the
reasons for rot and decay, but in food, not people. Joseph
was desperate for answers. He sought out the research
papers and began to read. The work was done by a chemist
named Louis Pasteur.

CHAPTER 8

The Frenchman and the Spoiled Wine

When a French winemaker needed help with a new wine he was creating from beets, he asked a local chemistry professor, Louis Pasteur, for help. While some of his vats of wine smelled fine, others began to stink, "spoiling into a slimy juice of useless sour ooze." Although people had been turning juice into wine for thousands of years, no one understood exactly how this process worked.

Pasteur traveled to the winery and peeked into the vats. The sour-smelling wine had a mysterious film coating its surface. He took samples and returned to his lab. First, he focused on the fresh-smelling wine. Under his micro-scope he saw globs of round yeast. He watched as they puffed and multiplied in number. They were alive! Pasteur determined that these tiny living organisms—or microbes—turned the juice into wine by a process called *fermentation*. Fermentation happened when yeast ate the sugar in the juice, turning it to alcohol.

In the sour wine sample, Pasteur spotted something different. Along with the yeast, he could see rod-shaped objects. This type of microbe changed the wine as well, but in a bad way. They made the wine slimy and undrinkable. He gave these microbes a name: germs (from the Latin word *germen,* meaning "bud" or "sprout").

Where did the germs come from? Did the spoiled wine *make* germs, through spontaneous generation? Pasteur didn't think so. He guessed that the germs were floating around in the air on particles of dust before they landed in the vat of wine. He created a simple experiment to find out if he was right.

Pasteur boiled some beef broth and poured it into

two glass flasks. Both flasks were globe-shaped with thin necks. One had a short, open neck. The other had a long, thin neck that curved like a swan's. While air could move in and out of both bottles, any dust and microbes would be trapped in the bend of the swan-neck flask. After several days, microbes grew in the short flask. The broth turned cloudy and started to stink. But the broth in the swan-neck flask stayed clear and fresh.

This experiment proved that it was germs *in* the air, not the air itself, that caused the broth to spoil. Pasteur had disproved the theory of spontaneous generation. If germs could simply be created by the nonliving broth, then both of the flasks would have grown cloudy and smelly.

Pasteur had a solution for the beet winemaker. If he heated his wine to 130 degrees Fahrenheit, the germs would be killed without changing the taste of the wine. Now the wine would not spoil too quickly, and it could be shipped to countries outside of France. Before long, word spread about this simple process.

Treat with Heat

The foods we eat and drink can make us sick if they contain harmful microbes. Today many foods—including milk, cheese, yogurt, butter, ice cream, eggs, juice, honey, nuts, beer, and vinegar—

undergo a brief heat treatment to kill bacteria and extend shelf life. To honor Pasteur, the process is called pasteurization.

In the early 1860s three of Pasteur's daughters died of typhoid fever. No one knew how the disease spread. Pasteur believed germs were to blame. But he was not a doctor. He had no medical training. He noted, "How I wish I had the special knowledge I need to launch myself wholeheartedly into the experimental study of one of the contagious diseases."

When Joseph finished reading about Pasteur's research, he felt a twinge of something new—hope. For so many years the mystery of hospital disease had left him in the dark. "A flood of light has been thrown on this most important subject."

CHAPTER 9

A Fortunate Stink

Tiny germs. In the air. Joseph's mind whirred with questions:

Were germs floating inside his hospital?

Could germs hurt his patients?

How could he get rid of germs?

To learn the answers, Joseph began by repeating Pasteur's experiments. Would he see the same results in Scotland as Pasteur saw in France?

Joseph placed two wineglasses on his kitchen table. Agnes grabbed her notebook. Instead of using beef broth for this experiment, Joseph wanted a substance from the human body. One that was easy to obtain. He chose urine. He boiled the urine and poured it into the glasses. Agnes took a small plate from the cupboard and covered one of the glasses. After three days, the uncovered glass of urine began to grow cloudy and stink. Joseph placed a drop of the liquid under his microscope. Tiny living objects wriggled before his eyes. After nine days, two woolly balls of fungus were visible to the naked eye. Agnes jotted down their observations: "The urine is now thronged with fungous growths of at least three different species; while the odour is highly offensive."

All the while, the covered glass of urine stayed clear and odor-free. Joseph's results were the same as Pasteur's: germs floated in the air, landed in the sample, and caused it to rot.

Joseph predicted that his patients' warm, moist wounds were the perfect landing spot for germs. Human skin was like the covered glass from his experiment. If skin stayed sealed—with no cuts or open wounds—germs could not get

inside. This explained why a broken bone healed easily. But an open fracture, where the broken bone tears through the skin, is like the uncovered glass. Germs are able to enter the body, grow, and multiply.

To help his patients, Joseph needed to kill these germs. But how? Pasteur had used heat to destroy germs in the beet wine. But Joseph couldn't heat people!

What about using a chemical on their wounds? Joseph thought, "Just as we destroy lice on the head of a child by applying a poison that causes no damage to the scalp, so, I believe we can use poisons on the wounds to destroy germs without injuring the soft tissues of the patient." But which chemical should he try?

In a nearby town, a stench wafted from fields irrigated with sewage water. After the fields were sprayed with a chemical solution, the terrible smell disappeared. More important, the cows that grazed on the treated land were not harmed. The chemical was called carbolic acid.

Joseph wondered what would happen if the carbolic

acid was used on his patients. Their wounds had a rotting smell, just like the fields. Could carbolic acid protect patients from hospital disease? To test his theory, Joseph needed a patient with an open wound.

CHAPTER 10

Catching a Break

On August 12, 1865, James Greenlees was rushed inside the hospital. The boy had been run over by a horse cart. Joseph examined the bruised, swollen leg. The bone poked through a jagged gash, which was now caked with dirt and dried blood. Joseph knew this injury all too well. It rarely healed, and the boy had a high chance of death from hospital disease. He prepared to amputate, as usual.

But Joseph hesitated. The boy was so young. Without his leg, how would he run and play? How would he one day find a job and make a living? Plus, there was no guarantee that an amputation would save his life. In the past two years, 46 percent of Joseph's patients died from hospital disease *after* their amputations.

Joseph made his decision.

After a deep breath of chloroform, the boy drifted to sleep. Instead of reaching for his surgical knife, Joseph grabbed a bottle of carbolic acid. He poured the solution into the wound, washing away bits of gravel and road filth and any germs that may have already landed inside the cut. Next Joseph soaked a strip of cloth in carbolic

acid and laid it over the wound. On top, he placed a piece of tinfoil to prevent the carbolic acid from evaporating. Finally, two wooden splints were strapped to either side of the broken leg.

Four days passed. It was time to check the wound. Would it be red and oozing? Rotting and stinking? Would Joseph need to amputate after all? He held his breath and slowly peeled back the bandage. The wound was completely clean! No pus or other signs of decay. A tiny bit of pink skin surrounded the cut. Joseph soaked a fresh piece of cloth with carbolic acid. This time he added a bit of olive oil to protect James's skin from the acid. Little by little, the wound closed. After six weeks, James walked out of the hospital on two sturdy legs.

Joseph had never seen anything like it. He wrote to his father about the boy, the horse cart, and the healing: "A most dangerous accident seems to have been entirely deprived of its dangerous element."

Joseph didn't have to wait long for another patient with an open fracture. Here was a man who'd been kicked by a horse. A woman who fell down the stairs. A boy whose arm was caught in a factory machine. A drunk man who jumped from a second-story window. And several more road accidents involving horse carts. These injured men, women, and children all received the carbolic acid treatment on their wounds.

In his first eleven cases, only one patient died (the cause was not related to Joseph's treatment). In a short period, the death rate from an open fracture dropped from 46 percent to 9 percent. Joseph was eager to share this new process with other doctors. Because his carbolic acid treatment plan prevented the deadly spread of septic germs that caused hospital disease, Joseph called the new method *antiseptic*.

He wrote a long paper filled with the details of his first eleven cases. It was published in a scientific journal for doctors and surgeons. Joseph began to use his antiseptic method not only for broken bones but for treating all types of cuts and sores. Hospital disease and gangrene disappeared from his wards. The germ-fighting techniques we use today—cleaning a wound, applying antibiotic ointment, and covering it with a bandage—got their start right here, more than 150 years ago.

Thrilled by the success, Joseph noted his treatment was "so simple and easy for *any* one to put in practice, that it really charms me."

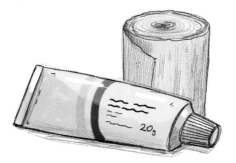

CHAPTER 11

Clearing the Air

Not every doctor was charmed by Joseph's new anti-septic method. They wrote angry letters back to the medical journal. Too complicated! Too time-consuming! It does not work! And many complained that Joseph wasn't the first person to use carbolic acid on wounds.

A few years earlier a doctor in France had written a seven-hundred-page book about carbolic acid. He stated it could do everything from preserving food to curing cancer. Joseph had not heard of the book. He defended his position: "I never intended to be so rash as to claim that I was the first surgeon who had in any way tried it. It was the principle and the method of its application that were new."

While the French doctor had written about carbolic acid, he hadn't given other doctors a step-by-step guide for its use. Joseph did. And he continued to fine-tune the process. Should the carbolic acid be stronger or diluted? Did foil, plaster, or oiled cloth protect the wound best? How often should the bandages be changed? Joseph collected data for each new attempt.

But other doctors complained that the instructions kept changing. They wrote more angry letters, calling the process "meddlesome" and "the latest toy of medical science." They said Joseph's system must not work if he had to change it so often. This criticism didn't stop Joseph. He continued to make improvements by following a set of steps, now known as the scientific method.

The Scientific Method

....

Joseph was not satisfied with outdated medical theories. To develop something better for his patients, he followed the process below. Gaining knowledge through observation and measurement began in ancient Greece more than twenty-five hundred years ago. Additional work from great thinkers such as Aristotle, Galileo, Newton, and Einstein helped to refine a set of steps that evolved into the scientific method we use today. Joseph knew important decisions must be based on data, not the opinions and beliefs of the time.

Observe: *Fields sprayed with carbolic acid stop the stink of sewage.*

Question: *Could carbolic acid protect patients from hospital disease?*

Form Hypothesis: Carbolic acid will speed healing and decrease the spread of hospital disease.

Experiment: Wash wounds with carbolic acid. Wrap in carbolic-soaked cloth. Cover with foil. Check at four days.

Analyze Results: Document size and color of wound. Measure amount of pus, if any.

Draw Conclusions: Carbolic acid supports wound healing and prevents the spread of hospital disease.

Report: Share findings with other doctors through demonstrations and written instructions.

Repeat: Mix a lower concentration of carbolic acid; repeat experiment.

Now that Joseph could protect wounds from harmful germs, he wanted to protect something else—the operating theater. Before a surgery began, he had everything wiped with carbolic acid. The table. The instruments. The thread for stitches. The patient's body. Even his own hands. But what about the germs floating in the air? Could he clean the air, too?

In 1870 Joseph invented a special contraption. It stood on tripod legs. When the handle was pumped—*hisssss*—a carbolic mist filled the room. Joseph reasoned that the spray would kill any germs that came in contact with his patients. But now operations took place in a thick fog. The spray got into eyes. It dripped from hair. It dried out hands. Joseph and his assistants tugged their coat collars to cover the skin on their necks. Although it was uncomfortable, Joseph insisted on using the spray for all of his surgeries. "A necessary evil . . . to attain a greater good."

Other doctors tried the carbolic spray. Few liked it. It was too tiring for the assistant to work the pump. The spray smelled bad. And they hated being soaked. A German doctor got so fed up with the process, he published a paper titled "Away with the Spray!" But the main reason so many doctors resisted Joseph's carbolic acid treatments? They still didn't believe in germs.

Older doctors were especially skeptical. How could something so tiny, something they couldn't see with their own eyes, kill a person? Many senior surgeons had never used a microscope. They didn't believe that germs caused disease. Or maybe they didn't want to believe that for years they'd been hurting patients more than help-ing them by allowing wounds

to become infected by these invisible creatures. While patients continued to writhe in agony, beg for their limbs, or die having babies, older doctors came up with their own plan for stopping the uncontrollable spread of hospital dis-ease—tear down unclean hospitals and rebuild them!

But Joseph's method was much more practical and afford-able. His results were impressive. Before carbolic treatments, nearly one out of every two surgical patients died. After the treatment was introduced, there were only six deaths in forty cases, dropping the death rate from 50 percent to 15 percent. The number of amputations dropped as well.

Joseph earned the support of younger doctors who were more open to a new way of thinking. And his medical students were eager to learn about germs and antiseptic techniques. While change was slow, Joseph continued on his germ-slaying quest: "I now perform an operation for the removal of a tumour, etc., with a totally different feeling from what I used to have: in fact, surgery is becoming a different thing altogether."

CHAPTER **12**

The Queen versus the United States

J oseph's research was briefly interrupted by some sad
news: his eighty-four-year-old father had died. Soon
after, his father-in-law, Dr. James Syme, died of complications from a stroke. Both men had been loving teachers and
loyal supporters of Joseph's work. They would be dearly
missed.

Joseph and Agnes moved back to Edinburgh. With Syme's
death, Joseph was now one of the top surgeons in Scotland.
He continued teaching medical students about germs, just
as he had in Glasgow. He continued writing papers about
his antiseptic method, with up-to-date instructions. But still
the leading doctors in nearby London were not convinced.

Without their support, he worried that his methods might never be fully accepted. Luckily a very important patient was about to give Joseph's method a royal try.

In 1871, while visiting her home in Scotland, Queen Victoria developed a sore throat and swelling in her left armpit. The queen found the orange-size lump painful and most undignified. When the local

- **Queen Victoria's abscess -**

doctor couldn't help, Joseph arrived with everything he needed to operate, including his carbolic spray pump.

He soaked his hands, instruments, and the queen's armpit in carbolic acid. An assistant worked the pump. The queen felt "dreadfully nervous," but she relaxed after a few whiffs of chloroform. Then Joseph carefully made an incision. Blood and pus flowed from the abscess. He cleaned the area and fashioned a small bit of tubing so any additional pus could drain away. Finally, he wrapped the wound with carbolic acid–soaked bandages and left the queen to rest. Within a few days, the wound healed and she felt much better. "A most disagreeable duty most agreeably performed," she noted in her journal.

When Joseph returned to his medical students, he declared, "I am the only man who has ever stuck a knife into the queen!" Word of the successful surgery spread. Slowly, the London doctors began to come around to Joseph's ways. Eager to continue this progress, he accepted an opportunity to convince more doctors in another important country— the United States.

In September 1876 Joseph sailed to Philadelphia for the Centennial Exhibition. The huge fair was planned to celebrate the one-hundred-year anniversary of the signing of the Declaration of Independence. Enormous crowds lined up to see the newest innovations in manufacturing, mining, transportation, and agriculture. Grand halls brimmed with artwork, plants, flowers, and inventions for the home.

Treats such as popcorn and root beer were tasted for the very first time.

The fair included the International Medical Congress, a meeting to share the latest in medical technology. Nearly five hundred doctors from around the world attended. It didn't take long for negative comments about Joseph's system to swirl. "Medical hocus pocus," said a doctor from Boston. A doctor from New York claimed there was no proof that germs caused disease. Still another remarked that his hospital was banned from using any of Joseph's

techniques. Convincing this crowd would not be easy!

All eyes followed Joseph as he approached the podium. He addressed the crowd in a friendly manner. He shared interesting stories about his research. He patiently answered questions. Although Joseph prepared a one-hour speech, he spoke for three and a half hours. "He *does* believe in antiseptic surgery," wrote one reporter. But afterward the head of the conference, Dr. Samuel Gross, stated, "Little, if any faith, is placed by any enlightened or experienced surgeon on this side of the Atlantic in the so-called treatment of Professor Lister."

CHAPTER 13

Operation Clean

Joseph wouldn't give up so easily. After the fair, he took a train trip around the Unites States, stopping at hospitals in San Francisco, Salt Lake City, Chicago, Boston, and New York. He performed surgeries and gave demonstrations to American doctors and medical students. He always emphasized the importance of his antiseptic system.

Slowly, hospitals in America began to change, too. Bloodstained wooden tables and wood-handled instruments were replaced with shiny metal. Wood floors were covered with easy-to-clean linoleum. Doctors hung up their crusty coats for the last time. They worked in clean linen shirts and operating gowns. Rubber gloves were introduced in 1894, almost twenty years after Joseph had toured the United States. Much later, toward the end of the 1920s, face masks were added to a surgeon's wardrobe.

Germs and Illness

Our bodies are covered, both inside and out, with trillions of tiny living organisms. While most of these microbes are helpful—especially with processes such as digestion and boosting our immune system—some types of bacteria and viruses can make us sick. The common term for these disease-causing microbes is germs. *Today's scientists call them* pathogens. *Pathogens can be found in the air or on surfaces, such as doorknobs, toilets, and countertops. They can be found in contaminated food and unclean water. If we breathe in pathogens, consume them in our food, or touch* an unclean surface and then touch our eyes, nose, or mouth, they enter our body. They can also enter through open wounds or insect bites. Once inside, pathogens begin to multiply, damaging the body's cells. Our immune system is signaled to begin fighting the invaders. You might have a fever, swelling, or rash—signs that your body is attacking the pathogens. But in some cases, our immune system alone isn't enough to ward off disease. In 1928 Alexander Fleming developed penicillin, the first antibiotic used to kill bacteria and treat certain infections. The first antivirals, drugs to kill viruses, were developed in the 1960s. Today the best way to avoid illness is to wash your hands frequently, avoid touching your face, and stay away from others who are sick.

It would take more than ten years for Joseph's ideas to be widely accepted. Perhaps the delay was partly due to Joseph's communication skills. For his whole life, he worried about his stutter. It made him nervous about giving speeches. He could hide his stutter if he spoke slowly and carefully. But his long-windedness was frustrating to some listeners. Also, Joseph didn't like to argue, so he may have had trouble speaking up to defend his antiseptic system.

When it came to writing, Joseph was known to ramble. He wrote in long sentences. He wasn't sure which details were most important. The meaning behind his word choices wasn't always clear. A friend once said, "Lister, in all his life, hardly ever succeeded in writing a good letter." Some doctors may have been right to call his new method confusing. But Joseph continued to practice his communication skills, giving lectures and writing papers for more than forty years.

Joseph's personality was his strength. Patients appreciated his kind and gentle manner. Once he treated a young girl with a badly injured knee. She clutched a ragged doll, its leg dangling by a thread. Joseph examined the doll and shook his head. "Very serious," he told the girl. He reached for a needle and carefully sewed the doll's leg back in place. Another successful surgery.

Joseph never raised his voice or lost his temper. He spoke calmly and focused on the facts. He was humble about his surgical skills. "I am honest and a lover of truth, which perhaps is as important as anything. As to *brilliant* talent I know I do not possess it: but I must try to make up as far as I can by perseverance." He spent late nights at his microscope. He made weekend visits to the recovery wards. His curiosity and dedication saved the lives of countless patients.

Gone Too Soon

· ·

Countless people have died because the surgery they needed could not be performed safely at that time in history. Without the ability to control infection, operations on the brain and the body's other organs were impossible. The figures listed below—and many others—might have lived longer if the work of Joseph Lister, and scientists before him, such as Ignaz Semmelweis, had been adopted sooner.

Notable Figure	Known For	Died	Age	Cause
Mary Anning	First female paleontologist	1847	47	Breast cancer
Mary Shelley	Author of *Frankenstein*	1851	53	Brain tumor

Notable Figure	Known For	Died	Age	Cause
Ada Lovelace	First computer programmer	1852	36	Uterine cancer
Crazy Horse	Lakota Sioux leader	1877	37	Stab wound
James Garfield	Twentieth US president	1881	49	Gunshot wound
Alice Roosevelt	Wife of Theodore Roosevelt	1884	22	Kidney failure
Emily Dickinson	Poet	1886	55	Kidney failure
Robert Louis Stevenson	Author of *Treasure Island*	1894	44	Bleeding in the brain

But Joseph couldn't have done it alone. Like most scientists, his discoveries were built upon the work of others, such as Louis Pasteur and, later, surgeon-scientist Robert Koch, who discovered that specific microbes caused specific diseases. Not *all* microbes were dangerous. While mostly yeasts and molds floated in the air, harmful bacteria were more likely found on doctors' hands and instruments (viruses had not been discovered yet). Joseph wasn't afraid to change his ways when this new data presented itself. He abandoned his carbolic spray pump after more than fifteen years of use. In its place, rigorous hand washing and instrument cleaning became routine.

CHAPTER 14

The Great Lifesaver

Joseph retired from medicine in 1893 after the death of Agnes, his wife and lab partner of thirty-seven years. He briefly paused his retirement in 1902, when King Edward VII came down with a fever and throbbing pain in his right side. The king needed his appendix removed, still a risky procedure at the time. Joseph did not conduct the surgery—he was nearly seventy-five years old—but he gave the other doctors precise instructions on the most current antiseptic techniques. The surgery went well and the king survived. Later he told Joseph, "I know that if it had not been for you and your work, I would not be here today."

Joseph earned many awards and medals. He was made

a lord by Queen Victoria. He was knighted by the king of Denmark. Statues were cast. Hospitals renamed. Still, one of his most recognizable honors may be found in humble bathroom cabinets. In 1879, after hearing Joseph speak in Philadelphia, Dr. Joseph Lawrence invented his own antiseptic solution. While it was first used to clean floors and treat dandruff, it later found success as a mouthwash. People still gargle with the stuff today: it's known as Listerine.

With the risk for infection reduced, no part of the body was off-limits for surgery. Lifesaving operations on the brain, heart, and lungs were now possible. Speed and strength were out. Care and precision took their place. Surgery results were no longer a lottery, decided by chance. Outdated theories were replaced by tested methods. Joseph Lister, the pioneering germ slayer, had changed surgery into a science.

Joseph Lister died on February 10, 1912, at the age of eighty-four. Unlike many medical pioneers, he was lucky to see his ideas accepted while he was still alive. Approval was slow at first. But there was one group who strongly believed in the antiseptic system from the very start—the patients who survived because of it.

After his death, a reporter for the *Times* of London wrote that Joseph "may be called the great life-saver." The newspaper estimated that Joseph had "saved more human lives than all the wars of the nineteenth century had sacrificed." Perhaps the value of Joseph's work is summed up best by

medical historian Harvey Graham: "It has been said that there are only two periods in the history of surgery—before Lister and after Lister."

Today Joseph Lister is remembered as "the Father of Modern Surgery."

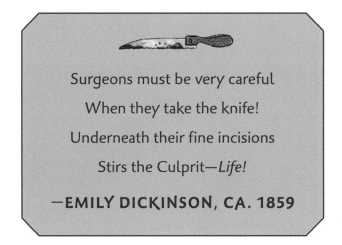

Surgeons must be very careful

When they take the knife!

Underneath their fine incisions

Stirs the Culprit—*Life!*

—EMILY DICKINSON, CA. 1859

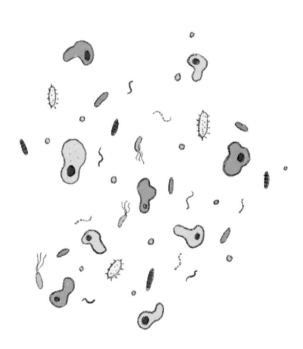

Photographs/Images

A page from Joseph's sketchbook at age seven.

Credit: Wellcome Collection

One of the oldest surviving operating theaters, built on the top floor of Saint Thomas's Hospital in London in 1822. The space now serves as a medical history museum. Note the unclean surgical tools, box of sawdust to soak up spilled blood, unwashed overcoat, and small bowl to rinse hands *after* surgery.

Credit: Old Operating Theatre Museum and Herb Garret

Case of amputation instruments used in Scotland, ca. 1750–1800.

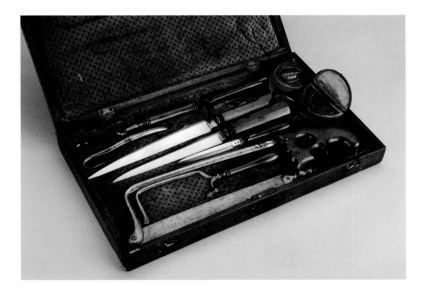

Credit: Wellcome Collection

Portrait of Joseph Lister at age twenty-eight, ca. 1855.

Credit: *Wellcome Collection*

The Gross Clinic by Thomas Eakins, 1875. This oil painting portrays a dark and crowded surgical theater in Philadelphia. As a nonbeliever in the existence of germs, Dr. Samuel Gross and his assistants operate in their day clothes with unwashed, ungloved hands. The wincing woman is believed to be the patient's mother.

Credit: Wikimedia Commons

The Agnew Clinic by Thomas Eakins, 1889. This oil paint-ing portrays a brighter operating theater, with Dr. David Agnew and staff in clean white coats and in the presence of a trained nurse. Some hygiene practices have improved in the fourteen years since Eakins painted *The Gross Clinic*.

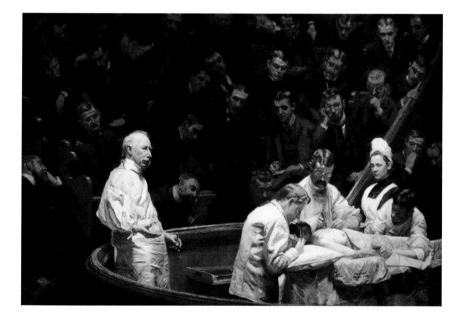

Credit: Wikimedia Commons

Time Line of Events

1827 Joseph Lister is born on April 5 in Essex, England, to Joseph Jackson and Isabella Lister.

- Joseph Lister -

1838 At eleven, Joseph is sent to boarding school about forty-five miles from home.

1844 At seventeen, Joseph enrolls at University College London, one of the few colleges that accepts Quakers.

1846 The first successful surgery under ether anesthesia takes place at Massachusetts General Hospital, Boston, when a patient has a tumor painlessly removed from his neck.

1846 Later that year, London's first ether surgery takes place when Robert Liston painlessly amputates a patient's leg.

- Robert Liston -

1847 Ignaz Semmelweis discovers the cause of childbed fever, a disease killing new mothers in Vienna, though his recommendation for hand washing is largely ignored.

- Ignaz Semmelweis -

1848 Joseph begins medical school.

1852 Joseph graduates from medical school with honors.

1853 Joseph moves to Edinburgh, Scotland, to complete his medical training with James Syme.

1856 Joseph marries Syme's daughter Agnes.

- James Syme -

1857 After accepting the role of assistant surgeon, Joseph conducts his first public operation.

1857 Florence Nightingale shows that sanitary hospital conditions drastically reduce death rates, based on her experience in a military hospital during the Crimean War.

- Florence Nightingale -

1860 Joseph and Agnes move fifty miles west to Glasgow when Joseph accepts a position at the Glasgow Royal Infirmary.

1860 Joseph is elected a fellow of the Royal Society for his research on inflammation.

1861 Louis Pasteur, a French chemist, discovers that germs cause living matter to decay. He publishes his germ theory, which identifies germs as the cause of disease.

- Louis Pasteur -

1862 Louis Pasteur invents a process using heat to kill harmful bacteria in milk, wine, and beer, now known as pasteurization.

1865   Joseph treats
eleven-year-old
James Greenlees
with carbolic acid.

1867   Joseph publishes
accounts of his
first eleven cases,
demonstrating
a lower rate of
death after using antiseptic techniques.

1869   Joseph's father dies.

1870   Joseph's father-in-law and mentor, James
Syme, dies.

1870   Robert Koch, a German physician, studies
microbes and their link to infectious
disease.

- Queen Victoria -

1871 Joseph uses antiseptic techniques to treat Queen Victoria for an abscess in her armpit.

1876 Joseph travels to the United States to speak at the International Medical Congress in Philadelphia.

1879 After hearing Joseph speak, Dr. Joseph Lawrence invents his own antiseptic solution, under the trade name Listerine. Today the mouthwash is promoted with the slogan "Kills germs that cause bad breath."

1886 Also inspired by Joseph's visit to America, Robert Wood Johnson and his brothers start a business to sell sterile surgical supplies. They name their company Johnson & Johnson.

1887   Surgical advancements on the brain, heart, lungs, and spine take place.

1892   Joseph travels to France to give a speech at Louis Pasteur's seventieth birthday celebration.

1893   After his wife, Agnes, dies, Joseph retires from medical practice.

1895   Joseph is made president of the Royal Society. He serves in this role until 1900.

1902   Joseph consults on an appendix surgery for King Edward VII.

1912   Joseph Lister dies on February 10, at the age of eighty-four, at his country home in Kent, England.

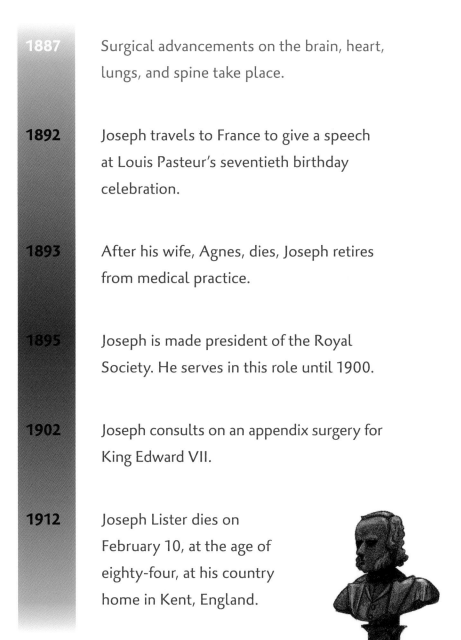

LISTER

1928 Sir Alexander Fleming develops the first antibiotic, penicillin. The drug is used to kill bacteria and treat certain diseases.

- Alexander Fleming -

1940 A strain of rod-shaped bacteria is given the name *Listeria* in Joseph's honor.

1950 The first superbugs, strains of bacteria that are resistant to or can no longer be killed by antibiotic medicine, are discovered.

2019 COVID-19, a highly contagious virus, first appears and goes on to infect more than 600 million and kill more than 6.7 million people worldwide (as of December 2022). Antiseptic routines, such as hand washing, remain as important as ever.

Today More than 350 million surgical procedures take place worldwide each year.

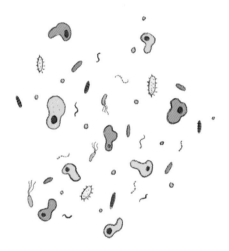

Glossary

abscess—a swollen area under the skin caused by a buildup of pus

amputation—the partial or complete removal of a body part, such as a finger, toe, hand, foot, arm, or leg

anatomy—the study of the body's parts

anesthesia—the inability to feel pain due to special drugs given before surgery

antibiotics—drugs that kill bacteria and are used to fight infections and diseases

antiseptic—free from or cleaned of germs and other harmful microbes

bacteria—one-celled microbes found nearly everywhere on earth; while many varieties of bacteria are helpful to humans, some cause disease

bloodletting—an outdated process in which a vein is cut to let blood drain out, thought to cure various illnesses

cadaver—a dead body donated for medical study

carbolic acid—a chemical mixture used to kill germs; also known as *phenol*

fermentation—the process by which sugar is turned into alcohol and carbon dioxide with the introduction of yeast

gangrene—the rotting of body tissue due to infection or lack of blood flow

germs—microbes that cause illnesses; also known as *pathogens*

germ theory—the idea that many diseases are caused by germs in the body

infection—the invasion of a body's tissue by germs, possibly causing pain, heat, redness, or swelling

infirmary—a place where sick or injured people receive care or treatment; a hospital

inflammation—redness, swelling, and pain that occurs when skin is rubbed, burned, or injured

maternity ward—the area in a hospital where babies are born and cared for

miasma theory—an outdated idea that diseases are caused by polluted, foul-smelling air

microbes—tiny living organisms that can only be seen with a microscope, including fungi, bacteria, and viruses

microscope—an instrument that uses lenses to make objects appear larger than they actually are

pathogens—microbes that cause illnesses; commonly referred to as *germs*

pus—a thick yellowish-white or greenish foul-smelling liquid produced by infected wounds

Quaker—a follower of a Christian religion devoted to peaceful principles

sanitary—characterized by cleanliness and health

sepsis—the body's extreme response to an infection, a potentially life-threatening condition that occurs when the body's response to an infection damages its own tissues

sewage—waste matter, including urine and feces, carried off by sewers

spontaneous generation—the idea that living organisms can be made from nonliving matter

surgeon—a doctor trained in cutting open the body to cure an injury or illness

ward—an area in a hospital for patients who need similar treatment

yeast—a type of microbe that causes fermentation and is used in baking bread and making alcoholic drinks

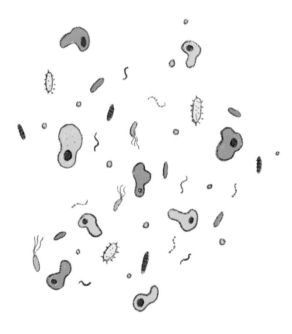

Source Notes

1. A Painful History

"houses of death": Fitzharris, *The Butchering Art*, p. 46.

2. The Boy and the Bones

"We get up at six": Fisher, *Joseph Lister*, p. 29.

"He finds no difficulty": Godlee, *Lord Lister*, p. 13.

"the boys do not even know": Fisher, *Joseph Lister,* p. 28.

"I got almost all the meat off": Godlee, p. 14.

"It looks just as if": Ibid.

"Do not tell Mary": Ibid.

3. The Quick or the Dead

"to let Nature do her own work": Godlee, *Lord Lister,* p. 14.

"the fastest knife in the West End": Laar, *Under the Knife,* p. 26.

"Time me, gentlemen!": Hollingham, *Blood and Guts,*
p. 36.

4. Easing the Pain

"lived in the world of his thoughts": Fisher, *Joseph Lister,*
p. 39.

"We are going to try a Yankee dodge": Ibid., p. 37.

"When are you going to begin?": Hollingham, *Blood and
Guts,* p. 63.

5. Hospital Disease

"mangle the living": Younker, *Bleed, Blister,* p. 48.

"good old hospital stink": Godlee, *Lord Lister,* p. 129.

"it seemed to be a lottery": Ibid., p. 19.

6. Agnes and the Frogs

"My present opportunities": Godlee, *Lord Lister,* p. 34.

"perfectly healthy": Ibid., p. 44.

"exceedingly quiet": Ibid.

"If the day were twice as long": Ibid., p. 30.

7. A Medical Mystery

"Whenever all, or nearly all": Godlee, *Lord Lister*, p. 198.

"I have often felt ashamed": Ibid., p. 197.

"a gentleman's hands are clean": Meigs, *On the Nature*, p. 104.

"The stiffer the coat": Gordon, *Great Medical Disasters*, p. 35.

"A soldier entering": Smith, *Infection Control*, p. 37.

8. The Frenchman and the Spoiled Wine

"spoiling into a slimy juice": Nuland, *Doctors*, p. 362.

"How I wish I had the special knowledge": Fitzharris, *The Butchering Art*, p. 158.

"A flood of light has been thrown": Lister, *On a New Method*, p. 327.

9. A Fortunate Stink

"The urine is now thronged": Lister, "Address on the Antiseptic System," p. 55.

"Just as we destroy lice": Lister, *Meeting of the International Medical Congress*, p. 328.

10. Catching a Break

"A most dangerous accident": Godlee, *Lord Lister*, p. 187.

"so simple and easy": Ibid., p. 189

11. Clearing the Air

"I never intended to be so rash": Godlee, *Lord Lister*, p. 206.

"meddlesome": Ibid., p. 207.

"the latest toy of medical science": Fitzharris, *The Butchering Art*, p. 191.

"A necessary evil": Godlee, *Lord Lister*, p. 284.

"Away with the Spray!": Ibid., p. 286.

"I now perform an operation": Ibid., p. 198.

12. The Queen versus the United States

"dreadfully nervous": Fisher, *Joseph Lister*, p. 193.

"A most disagreeable duty": Godlee, *Lord Lister*, p. 306.

"I am the only man": Fisher, *Joseph Lister*, p. 194.

"Medical hocus pocus": Fitzharris, *The Butchering Art*, p. 218.

"He does believe": Godlee, *Lord Lister*, p. 391.

"Little, if any faith": Fitzharris, *The Butchering Art*, p. 221.

13. Operation Clean

"Lister, in all his life": Fisher, *Joseph Lister*, p. 147.

"Very serious": Ibid., p. 86.

"I am honest": Godlee, *Lord Lister*, p. 41.

14. The Great Lifesaver

"I know that if it had not been": Fisher, *Joseph Lister*, p. 315.

"may be called the great": "Death of Lord Lister," *Times (of London)*, p. 9.

"saved more human lives": Ibid.

"It has been said": Graham, *The Story of Surgery*, p. 361.

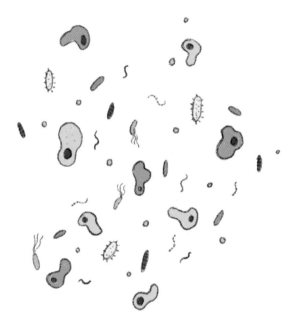

Selected Bibliography

"Death of Lord Lister." *Times* (London), February 12,
     1912, p. 9, col. 4; image copy, *thetimes.co.uk*
     (www.thetimes.co.uk/archive/find/Joseph+Lister
     /w:1912-02-11~1912-02-12: accessed September
     2020).

Fisher, Richard B. *Joseph Lister, 1827–1912.* New York:
     Stein and Day, 1977.

Fitzharris, Lindsey. *The Butchering Art: Joseph Lister's
     Quest to Transform the Grisly World of Victorian
     Medicine.* New York: Scientific American/Farrar,
     Straus and Giroux, 2017.

Fraser, W. Hamish. "Second City of the Empire: 1830s to
     1914." *The Glasgow Story.* June 2020.
     www.theglasgowstory.com.

Godlee, Sir Rickman John. *Lord Lister.* 2nd ed. London: Macmillan, 1918. Written by Joseph Lister's nephew, this biography was used as a primary source. It contains numerous letters written by Joseph to fellow surgeons and scientists as well as to his family and friends.

Gordon, Richard. *Great Medical Disasters.* Cornwall, UK, House of Stratus, 2001.

Graham, Harvey. *The Story of Surgery.* New York: Doubleday, Doran, 1939.

Hollingham, Richard. *Blood and Guts: A History of Surgery.* New York: St. Martin's Press, 2008.

Lister, Joseph. "An Address on the Antiseptic System of Treatment in Surgery." *British Medical Journal* 2, no. 394 (1868): 53–56.

———. "Meeting of the International Medical Congress." *Boston Medical and Surgical Journal* 95 (1876): p. 328.

———. "On the Antiseptic Principle in the Practice of Surgery." *British Medical Journal* 2, no. 351 (1867): 246–48.

———. "On the Early Stages of Inflammation." *Philosophical Transactions of the Royal Society of London* 148 (1858): 645–702.

———. "On a New Method of Treating Compound Fracture, Abscess, etc., with Observations on the Conditions of Suppuration." *Lancet* 89, no. 2272 (1867): 326–29.

Meigs, Charles. *On the Nature, Signs, and Treatment of Childbed Fevers*. Philadelphia: Blanchard and Lea, 1854. Digitized version accessed September 2020:

archive.org/details/onnaturesignstre1854meig /mode/2up.

Moore, Wendy. *The Knife Man: Blood, Body Snatching, and the Birth of Modern Surgery*. New York: Broadway Books, 2005.

Nuland, Sherwin B. *Doctors: The Biography of Medicine*. Ney York: Vintage Books, 1995.

Schneider, David. *The Invention of Surgery*. New York and London: Pegasus Books, 2020.
Smith, P. W. "Infection Control Through the Ages." *American Journal of Infection Control* 40, no. 1 (2012): 35–42.

Van de Laar, Arnold. *Under the Knife: The History of Surgery in 28 Remarkable Operations*. New York: St. Martin's Press, 2018.

For Young Readers

Platt, Richard. *Doctors Did What?!: The Weird History of Medicine*. Minnetonka, MN: Two-Can, 2006.

Townsend, John. *Bedpans, Blood & Bandages: A History of Hospitals*. Chicago: Raintree, 2006.

Younker, J. Marin. *Bleed, Blister, Puke, and Purge: The Dirty Secrets Behind Early American Medicine*. San Francisco: Zest Books, 2016.

Index

Note: Page references in *italics* indicate photographs and images.

frog experiments, 38–39

G

gangrene, 19, 33, 34, 47, 70
germs
    antiseptic treatment, 70
    carbolic acid treatment, 63–64
    discovery of, 56–59
    heat treatment, 58–59
    how they enter the body,
      61–63
    Lister's experiments on, 60–61
    name for disease-causing mi-
      crobes, 86
Glasgow, Scotland, 3–9, 44–45
Glasgow Royal Infirmary, 46
Greenlees, James, 1–2, 65–67
Gross, Samuel, 84, *102*

H

hand washing, 50, 53, 87, 92
healing process, 40, 46–47
hospital disease
    connection with inflammation,
      40
    death rates from, 37
    decrease in rates of, 70
    in Edinburgh hospital, 37
    in Glasgow hospital, 46–48
    origin of term, 34
    widespread nature of, 51–52
hospitals. *See also* hospital disease
    in 1600s and 1700s, 6

in America, 85–86
in early 1800s, 3, 6–9
in Edinburgh, 36–37
foul-smelling air in, 33
in Glasgow, 46
maternity ward diseases, 49–50
military, 52–53
mortality rates, 6

I

illness, 7–8, 86–87
immune system, 87
infections, 7, 9, 31
inflammation, 37–41
International Medical Congress,
    82–84

K

King Edward VII, 93
Koch, Robert, 92

L

Lawrence, Joseph, 94
Lister, Agnes, 41, 43, 93
Lister, Joseph, *101*
    attends medical school, 29–35
    attends university, 23
    awards and medals, 93–94
    boarding school, 13–14
    carbolic acid experiments,
      65–70